SEEDS OF TRUTH

DONALD J. WOODS

Printed in the United States of America

ISBN-978-1937979478

Cover design by Katy Acree

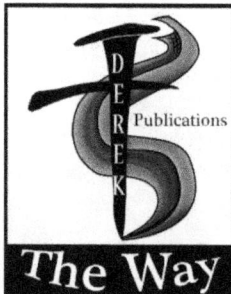

Derek Publications
www.derekpublications.com

Acknowledgments

First and foremost, I am profoundly and eternally grateful to my Lord and Savior Jesus Christ and my Heavenly Father for endowing me with the wisdom of His Spirit and Truth and idea for this book. Second, I am extremely appreciative to my wife, Mary for her godly love, patience, and encouragement. I also would like to acknowledge my pastor and spiritual mentor and coach, Rev. B.R. Hicks who has been a source of eternal encouragement, a fountain of wisdom, and loving spiritual mother. Rev. Hicks has provided an infinite wellspring of Truth to drink living water which has changed my life for eternity.

Purpose

The purpose of this book is to give the reader and Truth seeker a secret to growing in God and a spiritual boost and inspiration only Truth can give. Jesus, plainly declared, "And ye shall know the Truth and the Truth will make you free." (John 8:32 - KJV). Truth is liberating and enlightening. However, the work of Truth is a process. As we read, Jesus said the Truth will make you free. To make something is a process, not a single event or one-time experience.

Truth is not something you simply acquire cognitively and that's the end. Growing in Truth is a journey, a process, which begins with a seed or a point of light. And as the seed grows, it matures into its full potential according to God's design and creative work.

The interesting thing about a seed is though it is in the smallest form for the thing in which it will eventually grow to become, yet it contains all the DNA, essence, and potential needed to grow to full maturity. This is exciting to know even a seed of Truth holds great promise to mature and bring forth abundant fruit in our life. God's plan is for all His creation to mature. He only created seeds so they could grow. Nothing and no one should remain in a seed form or stage of growth indefinitely or beyond the customary season to progress and advance. Life, natural and spiritual, is built on this principle.

Truth frees you to walk in Jesus' footsteps, which can catapult one into new heights and deeper depths with God. Truth energizes, thrills, and encourages a wayfaring heart. It is a spiritual oasis, and a balm, which promotes healing from ignorance, doubt, and fear. Truth promotes spiritual growth and progress into higher realms of consciousness and the very reality of God. It is living and vibrant, awakening the human soul and spirit to greater awareness and existence. Truth is literally a guide and teacher, enabling its students to navigate the sometimes treacherous and tumultuous paths in life. Truth can be a constant companion if embraced and a sure comforter in times of loneliness, distress, and pain. Truth is the agent for growth and the means by which we expand and extend in all directions and in all levels of depths and heights of God.

Prologue

Seeds of Truth is a collection of personal thoughts from my journal as I have meditated, prayed, and reflected on various aspects of life in relation to spiritual Truths found in God's holy Word, the Bible. It is not a reflection on someone else's works or thoughts on the various topics presented.

Although I have included works of others for the purpose of expanding and expounding the Truth so the reader has the benefit of various perspectives, the majority of this work has come from my time and meditation with God. *Seeds of Truth* is inspired by God in my own personal life and relationship with Him, which has elevated my consciousness, enlightened my spirit, and raptured my soul to new heights and depths in the Word of God.

The Word of God is divinely rich in eternal sustenance and invaluable to a believer in Christ. As Rev. B.R. Hicks abundantly shared with her congregants for over 70 years, the next best thing to getting the Word of God for yourself is to share it with others. It is my sincere hope the light of Truth shine forth from these pages into the reader's heart and be a source of encouragement, excitement, inspiration, and motivation to grow in God to experience a deeper, more fulfilling relationship with the Lord Jesus Christ and our Heavenly Father.

All life and growth begins with a seed. Let me state that again, but in a different way to ensure a complete understanding of this wonderful, infinite spiritual principle. Life cannot begin until a seed is planted, properly nurtured, and grows to its highest and greatest potential to reach maturity. And within every seed is the full potential to become whatever form or state of life it was created to be whether human, animal, plant, etc.

Moreover, a seed needs sustenance from below the earth (soil, minerals, etc.) and from above the earth (sunshine, air, water, a nurturing human hand, etc.) to properly grow. And so it is spiritually.

For humans, even the body which is constructed of trillions of cells (the smallest biological structure in the body) is the seed of the entire human body. So, our bodies cannot grow and mature without the existence of a single cell, which is invisible to the naked human eye.

I think perhaps what is most confusing to Christians about spiritual seeds is the fact they are not visible, which makes it difficult to see the growth process until fruit has been born and become evident. Because we don't see outward signs of the visible fruits of Truth, we think we are doing something wrong or the process is not working. On the contrary, it may take hours, days, months, and even years of praying, studying, and worshipping God to even begin to see results of planting seeds of Truth in our hearts. We must not despair nor become discouraged in the process. God has a plan for spiritual growth, and we must follow the plan to be successful. And we will be successful if we cooperate and continue in The Way of Truth!

You must have a vision when planting seeds. You have to see the end result of the seed of Truth being planted. In the natural, if a farmer cannot envision his seeds producing a crop, he will never plant the first seed. So it is in our lives and handling the Truth of God. We must have a vision the Truth will come to fruition. For example, if I want to love more, I have to first see and believe I will love more. Then as I continue to nurture the seed of love, I will see signs of growth or increased love for myself and others.

The growth principle works. We just have to know how it works and cooperate with it.

Further proof of the seed principle, spiritually, is Jesus Christ who came in seed form in His earthly mother's womb. That holy seed had to grow to maturity inside the womb to become a baby. After birth, the Christ continued the growth process until He was mature enough to begin public ministry. Jesus, even though He is the divine Son of God, was subject to God's natural and spiritual laws of Truth. He could have easily bypassed the law of growth and matured from a fetus to a baby within a matter of seconds or bypass the womb experience all together; however, He didn't.

Being subject to the laws of nature, He gestated and matured in His mother's womb for 9 months like all humans. And He did not begin His public ministry as the Savior of mankind until he was 30 years old. Yet He was very patient with the process. This makes Him the perfect example of the seed principle of Truth. He did not try to circumvent the very laws and principles He represented and embodied. This should encourage us and help us choose to cooperate with God's divine plan and develop patience.

So, if the Son of God is subject to His own natural and spiritual laws of growth, how much are we, as humans, subject to these laws? Therefore, it behooves us to not only know how these laws work but more importantly cooperate with them. It is to this end, this book is written to help the reader understand God's natural and spiritual law of growth begins with a seed of Truth. With this knowledge, we should be grateful and excited to cooperate with the growth process and allow it to patiently work in our lives.

Not even the greatest of faith can supersede this principle. We simply cannot grow from a spiritual baby to a mature Christian overnight. It is a gradual, painstaking process, but it must begin with the recognition of a seed of Truth in whatever aspect or area of our lives. Then it is at that point, we begin to grow.

Often times, we want to accelerate achievement, rush spiritual and emotional development, or even instantly overcome some particular fault, habit, sin, or pain on our lives. We can be sincere and desperate, but until we begin the process with the right seed of Truth, the growth process simply will not start. And how disappointed are we when we think faith alone cannot speed or accelerate maturity. God will not violate His laws for the sake of our impatience and desires no matter how sincere.

Abraham, the father or common patriarch of the Abrahamic religions (Christianity, Judaism, and Islam) was promised by God he would make of him many nations of people. It was hundreds of years before this promise was to be fulfilled. Not even Abraham's outstanding faith shortened the process. The seed of Truth of God's promise had to grow to complete and full maturity, which took time.

So, where do we find the seeds of Truth to start growing in every area of our lives? They can be found in the Word of God, the source of all Truth and life. God has provided for every need for His creation. All works, according to Psalms 33:4, are done in truth: "For the word of the Lord is right; and all his works are done in truth." God begins all His works with a seed of Truth, which is a point of light. And the point of light expands and ever increases to shine on our pathway to grow in God.

Mark 4:26-33 expounds on the seed principle and

the fact the whole Kingdom of God is based on this principle:

> And he said, So is the kingdom of God, as if a man should cast seed into the ground;
>
> And should sleep, and rise night and day [implying the growth process], and the seed should spring and grow up, he knoweth not how.
>
> For the earth bringeth forth fruit of herself; first the blade, then the ear, after that the full corn in the ear.
>
> But when the fruit is brought forth, immediately he putteth in the sickle, because the harvest [maturity] is come.
>
> And he said, Whereunto shall we liken the kingdom of God? or with what comparison shall we compare it?
>
> It is like a grain of mustard seed, which, when it is sown in the earth, is less than all the seeds that be in the earth:
>
> But when it is sown, it groweth up, and becometh greater than all herbs, and shooteth out great branches; so that the fowls of the air may lodge under the shadow of it.
>
> And with many such parables spake he the word unto them, as they were able to hear it.

Finally, my sincere prayer is for this book to motivate the reader to cooperate with God's plan for spiritual growth in their life and to stir up a holy desire, zeal, and motivation to grow. There is nothing more thrilling than growth. When we grow, we get to experience the various levels and degrees of life and the vast, infinite realms of the Word of God, which directs us on our individual course of life referred to as the ***Derek Way*** in Hebrew.

Chapter One

_____

Gratitude

The Seed of Truth regarding gratitude is simply transformative. Once matured, gratitude is like a fully developed flower of the rarest bloom, emitting an intoxicating aroma, which tantalizes the soul and lifts the spirit of man from the lowest hell or pit to the highest depths and heights in God. The greatest expression of this principle was given by the Apostle Paul in 1 Thessalonians 5:18 when he said, "In every thing give thanks: for this is the will of God in Christ Jesus concerning you."

Understanding and getting the seed of truth regarding giving thanks or gratitude opens one's spiritual eyes to see God in absolutely everything. Without gratitude, one remains blind to the very essence, presence, will of God in every aspect of life. **It is exciting and such a blessed reassurance to know at the beginning, middle, and end of everything in my life is God's will for me.** To me, there is no greater Truth than this. So, despite pain or pleasure, rejection or acceptance, love or hate, God is in every situation and circumstance. Therefore, not only can I abide in every situation or station in my life at the moment, I can grow, bloom, and flourish. I can mature in this Truth!

The Apostle Paul shared his perspective on gratitude when he said, "Not that I speak in respect of want: for I have learned, in whatsoever state I am, therewith to be content (Philippians 4:11)." To be content is to be grateful, because you have sufficient means or substance in the current state to not only live but thrive. And to be malcontent is to be immature.

The Hebrew expression for *gratitude* is **hakarat hatov,** which literally means, "recognizing the good." The fact you do not acknowledge and proclaim the good in every situation or circumstance is evident you are immature and not faithfully practicing gratitude. A birth (a seed) in genuine gratitude is an awareness and consciousness there is always good in every circumstance or station in life. Gratitude is something we must practice the whole of our lives. It must be practiced in order to mature and to always recognize the good in everything, which happens to and for us.

So, how do I learn to recognize the good in everything? It is quite simple. *First*, we must seek God's will in the situation through prayer and meditation. God is faithful to answer our prayers. *Second*, when we have discovered the good, we need to immediately give

God thanks, because we know He will work everything out for good.

This principle really does work once you learn to practice it. At first, it may seem awkward, or even strange, but after doing it a few times, you will be amazed how effective and powerful it is in transforming any situation into a triumph spiritual or otherwise.

To give you a biblical example, let's examine the life of Joseph, a patriarch in the nation of Israel. Joseph's life story unfolds on the pages in the book of Genesis in the Bible. While we don't see the gratitude principle expressly written in the Genesis account, we know by principle Joseph heaped up gratitude and thanks while enslaved and imprisoned in Egypt.

Let's closely examine the evidence. First, in the whole account of Joseph's life, it was not recorded he complained or questioned his fate even once though hated by his brothers and falsely accused of rape, a crime for which he did not commit. Second, look at the status he attained in the household of Potiphar his slave master, Genesis 39:1 - 6; his rank in prison, Genesis 39:19 – 23; and ultimately his high political status in the nation of Egypt, Genesis 41:37 – 45.

If Joseph had not practiced gratitude, there is no way God could have used him to be and do all he accomplished to preserve the fledging nation of Israel and the known world at the time from famine and starvation. Without gratitude, Joseph would have been filled with anger, bitterness, distrust, hatred, and revenge for all the unjust and wicked plots and deeds committed against him. And God could not have used him if he was filled with these attitudes and dispositions to accomplish His high and holy will for His chosen people and the world.

Man in his fallen state is inherently ungrateful. But to transform our fallen nature and our outlook on life, we must start with a seed of gratitude--it is the first step in the process. We must be grateful Jesus made the ultimate sacrifice and paid the ultimate price for the salvation and redemption of mankind.

Because of its tremendous transforming power, gratitude is a force multiplier. Once I choose to be grateful, gratitude has an inherent ability, quality, and power to change any circumstance to something pleasant and agreeable once the good is recognized. As a personal example, I once lived in Southern California in the Los Angeles area. I hated the city I lived--the dry, arid climate was not something I enjoyed, being from the mid-West. I found nothing good about that place, pleasant or agreeable, until I finally recognized the good in being there. Once I became grateful, which is a choice, my attitude changed and the quality of my life instantaneously improved. I began to genuinely enjoy living in Southern California. When I changed by having gratitude, the desert became an oasis.

Gratitude causes disruption. In business speak, it is a disruptor. When sincerely practiced, it is a powerful force, which can literally change the course of events, but more importantly it changes your attitude and life —eternally. This seed of Truth begins the transformation to live a full and prosperous life God intended—naturally and spiritually.

Evidence you lack gratitude is complaining and murmuring. These are tall tale signs the seed of gratitude has not taken firm root and beginning to grow. But don't let the fact complaining and murmuring still exists in your life hinder you from forging ahead in the growth process. Begin to practice gratitude by diligently seeking good in everything. And when you find the good, you can be grateful and thankful. Then what was once a desert can be transformed into a spiritual oasis.

Do not just take my word for it. Let's see what others have to say about gratitude. Dietrich Bonhoeffer once said, "It is only with gratitude that life becomes rich!"

George Washington, the first President of the United States, on October 3, 1789 when he signed the Thanksgiving Proclamation introduced it by recognizing gratitude (thanksgiving) is not just a holiday but an attitude of the heart to be continuously practiced.

Whereas it is the duty of all Nations to acknowledge the providence of Almighty God, to obey his will, to be grateful for his benefits, and humbly to implore his protection and favor—and whereas both Houses of Congress have by their joint Committee requested me to recommend to the People of the United States a day of public thanksgiving and prayer to be observed by acknowledging with grateful heart the many signal favors of Almighty God especially by affording them an opportunity peaceably to establish a form of government for their safety and happiness (crosswalk.com).

The state of maturity for the Seed of Truth regarding Gratitude is always recognizing the good in everything; never murmur and complain; and be content in every station in life.

Start being grateful today and see how quickly your spiritual life grows and life in general is richer and sweeter! If you practice gratitude towards God and man, your life will be a blessing to God, you, and others.

Chapter Two

Mercy

The Seed of Truth regarding mercy changes how we see God, ourselves, and others. "Mercy is compassion in action," (unknown author). The Bible says, "For all have sinned, and come short of the glory of God[.]" Romans 3:23. Moreover, King David, speaking for himself, but this Truth applies to all mankind, declared in Psalm 51:1 – 5:

> Have mercy upon me, O God, according to thy lovingkindness: according unto the multitude of thy tender mercies blot out my transgressions.
>
> Wash me throughly from mine iniquity, and cleanse me from my sin.
>
> For I acknowledge my transgressions: and my sin is ever before me.
>
> Against thee, thee only, have I sinned, and done this evil in thy sight: that thou mightest be

justified when thou speakest, and be clear when thou judgest.

Behold, I was shapen in iniquity; and in sin did my mother conceive me.

We all break laws—man's and spiritual ones. And despite our best efforts, we manage to offend someone. For example, it is an offense to jay walk. But how many decent, otherwise law-abiding people jay walk in our city streets each day. The fact a person jay walks makes him or her an offender according to city ordinances. If the city exacted justice and punishment for each jay walking offense, the offender would receive a monetary fine or a jail sentence if the offense is life threatening or repetitive.

But mercy is the reason we overlook jay walking offenses unless it is so egregious as to cause a public safety hazard or nuisance. Even in this very simple example, we extend mercy to jay walkers, because we realize administering justice and punishment for every offense does not serve the greater good for society. Additionally, we recognize the offender still has potential to walk the streets without being a nuisance; and they can live a productive life despite the fact they break an ordinance by jay walking.

When taken in this context and from this perspective, mercy overrides justice in order to dispense goodness, lovingkindness, or redemption for a person who has broken a law or caused an offense.

This is precisely how God sees mankind and

instead of exacting justice for our offenses, He extends mercy even when we have offended Him in some manner and is deserving judgment.

Jesus demonstrated the principle of mercy when the religious leaders of His day brought a woman caught in the very act of adultery so He could judge and condemn her.

This incident is found in John 8:4 - 11:

They say unto him, Master, this woman was taken in adultery, in the very act.

Now Moses in the law commanded us, that such should be stoned: but what sayest thou?

This they said, tempting him, that they might have to accuse him. But Jesus stooped down, and with his finger wrote on the ground, as though he heard them not.

So when they continued asking him, he lifted up himself, and said unto them, He that is without sin among you, let him first cast a stone at her.

And again he stooped down, and wrote on the ground.

And they which heard it, being convicted by their own conscience, went out one by one, beginning at the eldest, even unto the last: and Jesus was left alone, and the woman standing in the midst.

When Jesus had lifted up himself, and saw none but the woman, he said unto her, Woman, where are those thine accusers? hath no man condemned thee?

She said, No man, Lord. And Jesus said unto
her, Neither do I condemn thee: go, and sin no
more.

Jesus, although He judged the woman's sin,
extended mercy to the poor sinner by telling her He
didn't condemn her but instructed her to live going
forward without practicing sin. In the dynamics of
this story, Jesus reset and renewed her life. Under the
Jewish Old Testament Law, the adulteress should have
been condemned to death. But Jesus' act of mercy
changed the dispensation of the Old Testament law at
that very moment, which condemned to die those
guilty of adultery, to the New Testament dispensation
of grace so she could walk in newness of life.

This is what mercy does for us and others: it
preserves, renews, and restores life! Therefore, we
should be eternally grateful for God's mercy and
always extend it to ourselves and others.

It is the nature of mercy to offer kindness and pity
in order to renew our relationship with God and
presumes the potential for future obedience and to
leading a productive life. Having mercy in our hearts
for ourselves and others can ever renew and rejuve-
nate our body, soul, and spirit from the offenses of sin.

*The state of maturity for the Seed of Truth regarding
Mercy is the power to overcome judging ourselves and others and
living a life of righteousness unto God.*

Ultimately, mercy is evidence God has not
condemned and punished a soul after judgment.
Mercy pushes back what we deserve and gives us what

we do not deserve, which is lovingkindness, pity, and acceptance. Mercy transforms wretchedness into righteousness once we surrender to God. This is a seed of Truth we need growing and living in our hearts each day.

Chapter Three

Shame

A sense of shame is a good moral trait to possess and aspire, especially in the progressive, secular, humanistic society we currently live. If a person lacks a healthy sense of shame, they do not have a sound Christian foundation. According to Rabbi Wein: "Without a sense of shame there can be no proper remorse for unjust and illegal behavior, nor can there be any hope for repentance and redressing wrongful behavior. The Hebrew words for shame and embarrassment appear often in our prayers and play a central role in our entreaties for Heaven's forgiveness. The sense of shame also appears throughout the words of the prophets of Israel and in the Psalms of David." (https://www.rabbiwein.com/blog/shame-and-shameful-180.html).

Shame is also evidence our hope is shaken in our eternal salvation and ties with God are broken. It is a sign we have not matured in hope. Paul expounds on this Truth in Romans 5:1 – 5:

> *Therefore being justified by faith, we have peace with God through our Lord Jesus Christ:*
>
> *By whom also we have access by faith into this grace wherein we stand, and rejoice in hope of the glory of God.*
>
> *And not only so, but we glory in tribulations also: knowing that tribulation worketh patience;*
>
> *And patience, experience; and experience, hope:*
>
> **And hope maketh not ashamed; because the love of God is shed abroad in our hearts by the Holy Ghost which is given unto us.**

Adam and Eve in the Garden of Eden is the best illustration of this Truth. After they disobeyed God by eating the fruit from the Tree of the Knowledge of Good and Evil, they were ashamed. And they allowed their shame to sever the sweet communion and relationship they previously had with God. In their shame, they hid themselves and sewed fig leaves to cover their nakedness of shame and sin.

The Greek word for *shame* (ashame) is (**pronounced kat-ahee-skhoo'-no**), which means to shame down, i.e. disgrace or (by implication) put to the blush; confound; dishonour; (be a-, make a-shame(-d).

Shame in the English dictionary means the painful feeling arising from the consciousness of something dishonorable, improper, ridiculous, etc., done by oneself or another. Moreover, shame is susceptibility to disgrace and regret.

Only an immature Christian will experience condemning shame. God never confounds or dishonors us. Yes, He humbles us through various afflictions (i.e., illness, loss, lack, etc.), but He does not shame us to degrade us. We experience shame by putting ourselves down due to a keen awareness of knowledge of a fault or error in our lives. However, a mature Christian abounds in hope, which sanctifies us from shame--a disturbed, painful feeling.

Like the Apostle Paul, I must learn to be abased and abound to be on the straight path. I equalize my life and my way when I have a good attitude in everything. In other words, accept and treat everything, situation, and person as a gift from God to help me grow in my moral development.

Thoughts and feelings of shame causes us to strive to earn God's approval and the approval of others. We do this because we see ourselves as a disappointment based on our choices and failures, which are unlike God.

This seed of Truth must start with being honest and stop seeking to earn approval on the basis of what we do or not do. We should no longer seek approval on the basis of performance but in the hope of God's love for us.

The state of maturity for the Seed of Truth regarding Shame is true repentance and a strong sense of hope, which will not allow shame to gain a stronghold, dominate our life, and sever our relationship with God.

A mature Christian abounds in steadfast hope of God's unwavering and unfailing love.

Chapter Four
_____

Intimacy

Intimacy is a level of connection between an individual and God and others built on trust, respect, and transparency. We cannot have true intimacy without Truth to lay bare and denude the spirit and soul. True intimacy is being vulnerable as a result of being stripped of all pretense and falsehood. True intimacy can only be achieved through purity and light. We become pure through the Blood of Jesus Christ and the light of His Word. Intimacy is not something to fear but rather to relish and embrace.

If you are still hiding faults and secrets about any aspect of your life, the seed of intimacy has not matured. I am not advocating public bearing of all faults, flaws, failures, and shortcomings, but rather a willingness to reveal and uncover those things about us unlike Christ mainly to God and others, as appropriate and necessary. I would only espouse sharing unChristlike attitudes, feelings, etc., to someone else after seeking God's wisdom and guidance how and when to share. Sharing a fault out of season can be detrimental to the one who shares and to the receiver.

As we gradually become honest with ourselves and become more willing to be vulnerable, the greater intimacy we can experience with God and others. A life filled with secrets is not a life well lived. Not only is it draining, self-defeating, and destructive, it is relegated to perpetually dwelling in the shadows of mediocracy and frankly defeat. More importantly, secrecy robs us of being our authentic self—it steals our true self-worth.

It's only when we have matured in intimacy, we can truly be our authentic self. Our authentic self is unlike any other person. Therefore, if we cannot readily see how different we are from others, we are not authentic. God made each of us uniquely different. And we should celebrate our own individual diversity.

We have a need and obligation to be true to ourself. Moreover, despite faults and failures, we have the right to be who we were created to be. Though not perfect, our life must shine as God intended. This is an important seed of Truth to grow so we can be comfortable with who we are and live our life to the fullest.

Fearing intimacy is counter to God's plan for man. Hebrews 4:13 reveals the truth about intimacy: "Neither is there any creature that is not manifest in his sight: but all things are naked and opened unto the eyes of him with whom we have to do." Since we cannot hide from God, why hide from ourselves and others?

If we ever needed a challenge to grow, this is one of the first areas to choose. Our lives cannot be full and happy without intimacy. We were created for intimacy albeit in various degrees, depending on our individual personality and gifting from God.

Theresa Dedmon offered this about intimacy: Just as teenagers can live in the same house as their parents, yet choose not to live "close" to them in partnership, so we can choose to be children of God, yet live very distant from God in our hearts. On the other hand, we can choose to have the closest partnership with Him, in which we know what He thinks, believes, and acts and what is important to Him. In this place of intimacy, we also discover just how close He wants to be with us (goodreads.com).

The state of maturity for the Seed of Truth regarding Intimacy is we notice our relationship with God and others grows where there is no hiding or withholding our true, authentic self.

Chapter Five
———————————

Songs of Deliverance

King David, in Psalm 32:7, opined, "....He [God] compass me about with songs of deliverance." What David declared in this Psalm is God used a song of praise and gratitude to surround and encapsulate him until God brought David to a place of deliverance or a haven from whatever bound, troubled, or oppressed him. A song of deliverance is a spiritual truth when recognized and understood, can bring about real encouragement, hope, and deliverance in a time of crisis, distress, or oppression.

At times in my life, only a song of deliverance liberated my broken, downtrodden spirit and soul and lifted me upon high, above my circumstances and enemies. A song or music can encourage or lift up the human spirit like no other, even compared to words of encouragement and hope from a friend.

To really understand this seed of Truth, it is necessary to define the word song, using the Hebrew language. The Word of God was originally written in the Hebrew language with some portions actually written in Aramaic. It is so clear in the Hebrew language songs of deliverance are ministers from God.

There are songs we sing to God and give Him the praise of our heart. Then there are songs God gives for the purpose of deliverance. And there is a distinct difference between the two.

Songs of deliverance comes from God to increase our faith and encourage us to go for Him in difficult times and circumstances.

Psalm 32 sets the stage for the purpose of a song of deliverance:

Blessed is he whose transgression is forgiven, whose sin is covered.

Blessed is the man unto whom the Lord imputeth not iniquity, and in whose spirit there is no guile.

When I kept silence, my bones waxed old through my roaring all the day long.

For day and night thy hand was heavy upon me: my moisture is turned into the drought of summer. Selah.

I acknowledged my sin unto thee, and mine iniquity have I not hid. I said, I will confess my transgressions unto the Lord; and thou forgavest the iniquity of my sin. Selah.

For this shall every one that is godly pray unto thee in a time when thou mayest be found: surely in the floods of great waters they shall not come nigh unto him.

Thou art my hiding place; thou shalt preserve me from trouble; thou shalt compass me about with songs of deliverance. Selah.

I will instruct thee and teach thee in the way which thou shalt go: I will guide thee with mine eye.

Be ye not as the horse, or as the mule, which have no understanding: whose mouth must be held in with bit and bridle, lest they come near unto thee.

Many sorrows shall be to the wicked: but he that trusteth in the Lord, mercy shall compass him about.

Be glad in the Lord, and rejoice, ye righteous: and shout for joy, all ye that are upright in heart.

In this Psalm, King David is distressed from his transgressions, sins, and iniquities. They overwhelmed him. But in verse 7, David said, "Thou art my hiding place; thou shalt preserve me from trouble; thou shalt compass me about with songs of deliverance. Selah."

I liken the song of deliverance for David and me to a capsule, tube, or chamber, which engulfs and surrounds to hide and protect from our fallen, human nature and spiritual enemies. In the midst of my failures, fleshly distresses, this is when God compasses me about with Songs of Deliverance.

The Hebrew word for *compass* is **cab'bab (pronounced saw'bab)**, which means to revolve, surround, fetch, lead, inclose, remove, and bring again among several other meanings.

To continue with defining the key words in this Psalm, let's also examine the words *songs* and *deliverance*. The word *songs* is **ron (pronounced rome)**, which means a shout (of deliverance): song. From its root word **raanan (pronounced raw' nan)** means to creak; to shout, triumph.

Deliverance in Hebrew is **pallet (pronounced pal'late)**, which means to escape and is from the root word **palat (pronounced paw'lat)**, which means deliverance; to slip out; escape, to remove; to walk; to carry away safe.

I have asked why does God give us songs of deliverance? It is because He knows our frailty, human weakness, and lack of spiritual growth to effectively use the Truth to deliver ourselves. The Word of God is sufficient to fight and win all spiritual battles. And Jesus clearly demonstrated this when confronted and accosted by Satan during His 40 days of fasting in complete solitude in the wilderness with His Father. You can read the full account in Matthew 4:1 - 11.

However, I will point out from these Scriptures, Jesus was so effective using the Word of God to fight Satan, Satan had to depart from Him, realizing He could not prevail against the Truth.

Because we are not like Jesus and not as skilled at using the Truth to fight the lies of Satan, at times, God gives songs of deliverance to fight for us in order to continue our spiritual journey. Often, we can find ourselves stagnant in the growth process and our journey. If we don't know how to use the Truth, we cannot prevail and progress.

Since this is the case, God gives us songs of deliverance to help us defeat our own negative attitudes, the carnal, human nature, and Satan. Also, He wants us to serve Him and in order to accomplish this, He has to deliver us from the place we are stuck or bound and bring us onto Himself. And most importantly, He gives us songs of deliverance to open our hearts to the Word so we can learn to use it more effectively in the next spiritual battle.

This is a strange concept for some so let me illustrate the point I am trying to make with this seed of Truth. Several years ago I had to drive alone for over 400 miles south to be with my family. At that particular time, I was completely mentally and physically exhausted and very discouraged. I had finished a very long, arduous week at work which left me fatigued, stressed, and depressed.

The Spirit of God impressed upon me to listen to this one particular song, and I literally listened to that song of deliverance the entire trip, which was about 6 1/2 hours. The Spirit of God, through the song of deliverance, gave me strength and energy to make it to my final destination and in record time! How do I know it was the song of deliverance? I had a strength that did not come from within me but from above. It was as if I was floating on a cloud in the midst of my fatigue and distress.

There was another time when traveling on business to Chicago. I had retired to my hotel after a long day of travel and work. And at this particular time, I was feeling hopeless and helpless. I could not see my way out of the cloud and fog of depression. I could not reason my way out of this situation. I was stuck and not moving forward—I was at the end of my road so to speak. Then I heard the lyrics of a song, "I shall live and not die." The Spirit of God, through the lyrics of the song, "removed" me from the pit I was in, and I was able to "walk" forward in my life. I was so encouraged after listening to the song. It was as if my life began anew—I was delivered!

A lack of maturity will not seek a song of deliverance in the time of distress and trouble. It is not until you begin to grow in this Truth music and songs take on a whole new purpose and function. God gave us music and song to lift us up onto Him--spiritually. And to take us to a higher realm of Truth, love, and His presence. If we do not understand this, we abuse music and song for our selfish purposes and consume it in our lustful thoughts and deeds, seeking temporary pleasure.

The state of maturity for the Seed of Truth regarding Songs of Deliverance is recognizing they serve as ministers to take us on in the face of distress due to our carnal will, the fleshly human nature, and Satan. They take us to the foot of the Cross of Calvary to worship the Savior and to surrender to continue our spiritual journey.

May we grow to maturity to use the things of God as He intended so we can be more like Jesus Christ.

Chapter Six

Growing in God's Image

Growing in God's image or being a man or woman of God is more about identity than a position or ministry in the body of Christ (i.e., the church). A person of God is one who represents God by demonstrating His values and virtues, which are love, peace, faith, mercy, grace, etc. A person of God is an agent to carry out God's will and purpose on earth. It is one who is like God in behavior, thoughts, and feelings. It is more than a ministry, but a way of life.

We need not look beyond the book of Genesis to clearly understands God's purpose for mankind. Genesis 1:27 says, "So God created man in his own image, in the image of God created he him; male and female created he them." Based on God's original design and plan for man, we are all called to be a person of God. Therefore, we should all strive to be one who does the will of God and pleases Him.

If we do not desire or strive to be like God every

day, we are immature and have need of growth. If we live our own lives without giving thought to growing in God's image and character of love, mercy, holiness, etc., we are immature.

God's nature and character is embodied in the Ten Commandments. The Commandments were given to preserve life and for man to manifest God's nature in all his life's activities.

As part of this process of growing in God's image, we are commanded to love like God:

Matthew 22:37 - 40
Jesus said unto him, Thou shalt love the Lord thy God with all thy heart, and with all thy soul, and with all thy mind.
This is the first and great commandment.
And the second is like unto it, Thou shalt love thy neighbour as thyself.
On these two commandments hang all the law and the prophets.

We are commanded to be holy like God:

Leviticus 20:7
Sanctify yourselves therefore, and be ye holy: for I am the Lord your God.

We are commanded to show mercy, true judgment, and compassion like God:

Zechariah 7:8-10

> And the word of the Lord came unto Zechariah, saying,
>
> Thus speaketh the Lord of hosts, saying, Execute true judgment, and shew mercy and compassions every man to his brother:
>
> And oppress not the widow, nor the fatherless, the stranger, nor the poor; and let none of you imagine evil against his brother in your heart.

We are commanded to avoid evil and seek peace like God:

1 Peter 3:11-12

> Let him eschew evil, and do good; let him seek peace, and ensue it.
>
> For the eyes of the Lord are over the righteous, and his ears are open unto their prayers: but the face of the Lord is against them that do evil.

This seed of Truth begins with a desire and a choice to live for God. Once the desire takes root, the wheels are set in motion to grow into maturity.

The state of maturity for the Seed of Truth Regarding God's Image in us is seeking to do God's will and pleasing Him by taking on His holy, divine nature.

Chapter Seven
—————————

Our Heavenly Father

Our Heavenly Father is so wise! As we grow in the Truth and knowledge of Him, we better understand how we should relate to Him. From the beginning of time, it was God's plan for earthly fathers to be a picture of Him so we ultimately learn how to relate to, love, and respect our Heavenly Father. Paul helped explain this principle in Romans 1:20 when he said, the natural things are a type of the spiritual or heavenly things. This also applies to earthly fathers as a type of the Heavenly Father. Since this is the case, earthly fathers should behave in a manner to teach and demonstrate to their children how to properly relate to their Heavenly Father.

Unfortunately, for most of us, this was not the case. As a result, we have developed a distorted view of the Heavenly Father, which has resulted in a chasm and relationship deficit. But no need to despair. As the seed of Truth regarding the Heavenly Father grows, we can learn to restore and develop the proper relationship.

This seed of Truth begins with understanding the role of earthly fathers to teach children about the Heavenly Father. As we grow and mature, we no longer doubt anything our Heavenly Father allows to happen in our lives, because we grow up knowing everything is for our good and His eternal glory. 1 Thessalonians 5:18 (AMP) makes this abundantly clear, "Thank [God] in everything—no matter what the circumstances may be, be thankful and give thanks; for this is the will of God for you [who are] in Christ Jesus [the Revealer and Mediator of that will]." However, we cannot come to this conclusion if we do not see God as our father. This level of unbridled, unfettered trust is only relegated to fathers.

When Jesus taught his disciples to pray in Matthew 6:9 – 13 (KJV), He did more than teach them how to pray. He gave them a profound revelation regarding the Heavenly Father: His nature and how to relate to Him. His model prayer started, "Our father, which art in heaven..." affirming the Truth God is our Heavenly Father and all prayers and relationships start with Him. The rest of the prayer reveals how we are to relate to the Heavenly Father. I will explain this further below.

First, His name is holy—sanctified and pure. His holiness separates unto life and wholeness. His holy name is not marred and distorted by sin and lies. To really appreciate and love His name, we must recognize, celebrate, and be separated unto His holiness (Leviticus 20: 7).

Second, His kingdom (rule and authority) is to come within us. Jesus said the kingdom of God is within you (Luke 17: 21). It is an inward kingdom through Jesus Christ. A kingdom has a king, and God is the king of our kingdom. In Luke 12: 31, we are encouraged to seek the kingdom of God above all else.

Third, His will must be done in our lives both in earth and in heaven. Like a good father, His will is to prosper us. Refer to Nehemiah 2:20 and Genesis 39:3.

Fourth, The Heavenly Father gives daily bread to strengthen us to take on His nature, abide in His kingdom, and walk in His will.

Fifth, we must learn to forgive as the Father forgives us. The story about the prodigal son is an excellent example of forgiveness (Luke 15:11 - 32). Despite how far we or someone else strays from the Heavenly Father, we must forgive, welcome them back into the family, and celebrate their return to spiritual life in Christ Jesus.

Sixth, the Heavenly Father will not lead us into temptation. We are led into temptation by our own lust, which ensnares us and we fall into temptation (James 1:12 - 15).

Seventh, The kingdom, power, and glory all belong to the Heavenly Father. We do well to understand this and not usurp the Father's authority in our lives. As corrupt, mortal human beings, we want authority over our life so we can rule, exercise power, and heap glory on ourselves. If we are to properly relate to our Heavenly Father, we must lay down our will and authority for our lives and willingly surrender our kingdom to him. And when we do, He can truly reign and all glory will truly belong to Him.

What blessed assurance we have in our Heavenly Father! However, as we grow from a seedling to a mature tree in this Truth, we often falter on this concept. Our doubts and fears whether God has good intentions regarding us cloud our thinking and feelings, which produces distrust. So, often when faced with temptation, adversity, lack, or pain, we immediately doubt our Heavenly Father. The doubt stems from not having grown sufficiently to trust in our relationship with Him as a father to meet our every need and to make everything work for our good.

This principle is particularly difficult and even troubling for those who did not have a good relationship with their earthly father. Without a solid relationship with a natural father, it is very challenging to understand, appreciate, or even seek a relationship with the Heavenly Father.

When we mature in our relationship with the Heavenly Father, we no longer doubt, nor fear, anything, because He is in control, and He will provide for every need. If this is not our current mindset and attitude, then we have need for further growth.

How do we grow in our relationship with the Heavenly Father? It's quite simple really. It starts with a small measure (or seed) of trust and confidence in

His holy nature until it grows to maturity. God is too holy, righteous, just, merciful, and loving to allow even the smallest pain or misfortune befall us, which will not foster a deeper, higher, and broader relationship with Himself.

He often uses pain to help us grow in our relationship. Pain and suffering are excellent instructors in the way of righteousness and true holiness. King David, the psalmist of all psalmists, reveals the key to growing in our relationship with the Heavenly Father in pain and suffering, which is praise and gratitude for all things. According to King David, praise and gratitude are powerful forces to spur spiritual growth in every area of our lives, because in the midst of praise and gratitude we find loving trust and confidence, which helps the heart grow spiritually and forges a deeper relationship with the Heavenly Father.

When confronted with temptations, doubts, and circumstances which threatens to make us doubt our Heavenly Father, we must learn to immediately give thanks and praise for everything as a witness and demonstration we trust and have confidence in Him.

The state of maturity for the Seed of Truth regarding Our Heavenly Father is we have a greater realization we can always trust Him to provide for our every need--no exceptions!

Chapter Eight

Prayer

Prayer is a spiritual force—bold, daring, and indomitable. And as we pray, we instantly move the hand of God, because He wants nothing more than to converse with, relate to, and respond to every need of His creation. To think contrary to this is to rail accusations against God's holy, divine nature.

According to an old English proverb, "Many things are lost for want of asking." The biggest reason our prayers are not answered is found in James 4: 3 AMP, "[Or] you do as [God for them] and yet fail to receive, because you ask with wrong purpose and evil, selfish motives. Your intention is, [when you get what you desire] to spend it in sensual pleasures."

Prayer is much more than just communicating and dictating our wish list to God for things we desire: it is a means to commune and have companionship with God. If you are lonely, just pray, and you will be amazed how God answers and responds by joining

Himself to you. Our problem is we have not learned how God speaks to us, which is through different channels and means and mostly from sources we don't expect or anticipate. The key to hearing or seeing God's answers to our prayers is humility and patience. We must be patient to wait and humble enough to hear and listen to the voice of God speaking through people, circumstances, and situations.

The prophet Elijah is a great example of this principle. In his moment of desperation and despair, fleeing the wrath of Jezebel, the wife of Ahab a Jewish king, God did not respond to Elijah's prayers in an obvious and blatant way. Instead, God came to him in a still, small voice, which took patience and humility to wait for and to hear it.

1 Kings 19:11 - 15 (KJV):

And he said, Go forth, and stand upon the mount before the Lord. And, behold, the Lord passed by, and a great and strong wind rent the mountains, and brake in pieces the rocks before the Lord; but the Lord was not in the wind: and after the wind an earthquake; but the Lord was not in the earthquake:

And after the earthquake a fire; but the Lord was not in the fire: and after the fire a still voice.

And it was so, when Elijah heard it, that he wrapped his face in his mantle, and went out, and stood in the entering in of the cave. And, behold, there came a voice unto him, and said, What doest thou here, Elijah?

And he said, I have been very jealous for the
Lord God of hosts: because the children of Israel
have forsaken thy covenant, thrown down thine
altars, and slain thy prophets with the sword; and
I, even I only, am left; and they seek my life, to
take it away.

And the Lord said unto him, Go, return on thy
way to the wilderness of Damascus: and when
thou comest, anoint Hazael to be king over Syria.

After Elijah recognized and accepted the medium
of God's response to his prayer (the still small voice in
the midst of his tumultuous situation), the Lord
instantly gave him instructions to follow His will.
Waiting on God is not detrimental to us, but rather as
Evagrius Ponticus (a Christian monk and one of the
most influential theologians in the late fourth-century
church) pointedly stated, "Do not be troubled if you
do not immediately receive from God what you ask
him; for he desires to do something even greater for
you, while you cling to him in prayer."

Wouldn't it be rude and show an utter lack of
caring and attention to our lives if God ignored our
prayers? Does that sound like a loving and caring God
to you? Of course not. The fact we want instant grati-
fication when we pray is because we do not understand the nature and purpose of prayer. It is also a
sign we are immature. Just because we don't see God's
invisible hand moving on our behalf the moment we
utter the first word of our prayer, does not mean He is
not listening nor working on our behalf. God is too

holy, righteous, just, and loving to ignore His children despite their level of maturity or spiritual condition.

One thing we can be certain is our Heavenly Father is not unloving and unconcerned about the affairs of our lives. In the book of Genesis in the Old Testament, God walked with man in the cool of the day. God had a special appointment to talk with man every day. So, it should be in the life of each Christian. Since God is so interested in every aspect of our lives, our prayer should be more than making a request of God for something. Instead it should be a discourse where there is an exchange of ideas, concerns, thoughts, feelings, praise, gratitude, and appreciation. It is through prayer we can instantly connect and fellowship with God.

As we mature as Christians, our prayers should evolve more into praise and thanksgiving than asking for things. Asking should be secondary, because our Heavenly Father already knows what we need before we even ask. What is more important is to demonstrate faith by praising and thanking Him in advance for whatever you're asking, because He has already heard your prayer. We can rest assured, as a benevolent Father, He will meet the need based on His will and plan for our lives.

Spiritual growth in prayer is a process. As an immature Christian, we often spend most of our time asking for things or pleading for something to work in our favor, because we have not learned the true purpose of prayer and how it is to be used to reach the ears and heart of our Heavenly Father. As we grow, we learn to ask less and to praise and listen more to Him so we can perform His will. Jesus said He always does the will of His Father. And as you grow to full maturity, prayer is a pleasure. It is entirely relegated to seeking His will for your life. The only asking is to lay a need before Him for guidance and to ensure the answer will align with His holy will and purpose. Mature praying is more about praise than anything else. It is true fellowship and mutual admiration. As you pour out love and gratitude to Him, He reciprocates by pouring out more of His love and gratitude upon you while meeting our needs.

Studying the Word of God and meditation is a great way to enter into a deeper state of communion with God. Meditation, when done through the Spirit of God, is a deep connection and exchange of Truth and spiritual energy which helps you grow. In Isaiah 1:18, God said, "Come now, let us reason together..." Prayer is an opportunity to reason with God. Abraham demonstrated this principle when he prayed God spare the few righteous souls in the cities of Sodom and Gomorrah from impending judgment and utter doom. Abraham used prayer to reason with God. Since Abraham's prayers came from his heart of love and mercy, God granted His prayer and the righteous were indeed spared.

We can have the same experience as Abraham if we pray in the right spirit and frame of mind, which is to establish a greater connection and fellowship with God to take on His divine nature. The whole purpose of prayer is to connect with God to learn how to grow in Him and how to please His heart. If we pray for any other reason than for fellowship or to please Him, we are immature and in need of further growth. The evidence you have matured in prayer is the amount of praise and admiration and seeking His will verses the amount of time asking for things to satisfy yourself and others.

Even if we are praying for a noble cause, and if it is not for the will of God, then we ask amiss as previously mentioned from James 4:3, "Ye ask, and receive not, because ye ask amiss, that ye may consume it upon your lusts." If our prayers are selfish, even when praying for others, we can expect not to receive what we asked as we just saw in James.

I encourage the reader to grow in prayer. Like Adam in the Garden of Eden, God has an appointment to talk and commune with you through prayer. Start by setting aside some time each day to pray and meditate.

The state of maturity for the Seed of Truth regarding Prayer is a sincere desire to connect and fellowship with God for the sole purpose to bring pleasure to Him and doing His will.

_____

Chapter Nine

Birthright

In the simplest meaning, a birthright (entitlement) is a right or privilege of some kind bestowed at birth. It can be a moral or natural right or a certain type of privilege or possession. For example, from a biblical standpoint, a birthright is bestowed upon the eldest son to lead the family after the father dies. In another sense, a birthright can be access to affordable education in certain countries. However, a birthright is not something you earn or merit. You are simply born with or entitled to it. It is easy to distort this Truth because performance is such a big part of our motivation and attitude regarding everyday life from relationships, careers, sports, etc. We measure success by results, which is driven by performance.

Well, with God we have a birthright not based on performance. Instead we have been freely granted access to God's divine, holy presence and nature simply because we exist. However, we must grow and mature in this awareness. In our infancy stage of growth, we are quick to separate or divorce ourselves from the things of God because we think and feel we do not deserve them. Consequently, when we fail in some way, we forfeit our birthright in exchange for failure.

We lack maturity when we think our faults, failures, sins, or external forces and powers can disinherit or separate us from God's love and presence. In Romans 8:35 - 39, we learn nothing can separate us from our birthright of God's love:

> Who shall separate us from the love of Christ? shall tribulation, or distress, or persecution, or famine, or nakedness, or peril, or sword?
>
> As it is written, For thy sake we are killed all the day long; we are accounted as sheep for the slaughter.
>
> Nay, in all these things we are more than conquerors through him that loved us.
>
> For I am persuaded, that neither death, nor life, nor angels, nor principalities, nor powers, nor things present, nor things to come,
>
> Nor height, nor depth, nor any other creature, shall be able to separate us from the love of God, which is in Christ Jesus our Lord.

Even though we have an irrevocable, irreversible, immutable birthright, our responsibility is to cherish it and broaden our awareness of this Truth as we encounter people, things, and circumstances in our lives. Our birthright grants access to such great love—the love of God. So, may we continue to grow in greater awareness of and belief in our God-given birthright.

Entitlements, from a human perspective, can change and often do, depending on political or social forces. But our Heavenly Father never changes. He is the same yesterday, today, and forever. Additionally, we find God's natural and spiritual gifts or talents and ministerial or administrative callings are immutable (i.e., they cannot be changed despite my spiritual and moral condition or station in life (Romans 11: 29 KJV). This should encourage us to no end to think we have a birthright, which guarantees our position with God.

The state of maturity for the Seed of Truth regarding Our Birthright is recognizing there is nothing we can do to merit God's love, favor, and presence. And the gifts and callings on our life are irrevocable. Moreover, these things are not something earned. They are a birthright and nothing can separate us from God's love and His calling, plans, and purpose for us.

Chapter Ten

Words

Words reveal a lot about the person speaking them. They reveal character, attitude, and, moreover, the condition of the heart. Words convey meaning, reveal emotions, passions, desires, and motives. How many words (good or bad) have you heard which still affect your life or helped shape who you have become today or perhaps for eternity?

"You do not really understand the significance of words until you realize that the first words that human ears ever heard were not the words of another human being, but the words of God! The value of every piece of human communication is rooted in the fact that God speaks." (Paul David Tripp, *War of Words: Getting to the Heart of Your Communication Struggles*).

In our immaturity, we use words very carelessly without regard to the permanent or eternal impact or effects they create. The Psalmist cried, "Let the words of my mouth, and the meditation of my heart, be acceptable in thy sight, O LORD my strength and my redeemer." (Psalm 19:14). We should have the same cry and desire as King David for every word spoken.

In the Hebrew language, there are two distinct words and meanings for *"word"*: **Dabar (pronounced daw'baw) and amar (pronounced aw'mar)**. I will focus on the definition of the former, **dabar**, which means to arrange; to subdue; answer, appoint, bid, command, commune, declare, destroy, give, name, promise, pronounce, and rehearse. Also, by implication it means a cause; affair; chronicles; disease; power; promise; provision, and purpose.

As the meaning implies, a word is a cause. Words cause things to happen--good or bad; honorable or dishonorable. Words initiate, motivate, influence, and prompt people to act in a certain manner. How many times have politicians used words to get people to vote or cause division on an issue? Words can even spark a war if so desired.

We can carry on an affair with our words. What do I mean? Some people simply love to hear themselves talk. They are enthralled with their own speech. And at times, we are all guilty of carrying on an affair with our words or the words of others. We like to peddle ideas and thoughts in hopes we can influence things or get people to act or behave a certain way.

Words reveals knowledge; they are a book (chronicle) of what we believe, understand, know, and live our lives.

Words are counsel for good or bad: "The entrance

of thy words giveth light; it giveth understanding unto the simple" (Psalm 119:130).

Words can also be a disease. Our thoughts (non-verbal speech) can be cancerous and a plague to our body, soul, and spirit. "The words of a talebearer are as wounds, and they go down into the innermost parts of the belly" (Proverbs 18:8).

Our words convey our motives, desires, feelings, and intentions--they reveal what is hidden. Therefore, because words and thoughts are intimately connected, we must be very careful about how we think, and especially about how we esteem ourselves and others.

Rabbi Meir Kagan wrote the foundational principle of guarding our speech is to always judge others in the best possible light, which entails recognizing the good in others and choosing to see with a good eye. He further believes, "It is better to judge favorably—even if we are in error—than it is to judge critically even if we are telling the truth. Our judgments carry great weight in heaven. The words we say, whether good or bad, call for a response in the spiritual realm."

We must learn to listen to the words of our heart and understand they are "things" (or substance), defining the course of your life. Our inward motive determines your thinking, which in turn affects the way we act and use words.

This is why, in Proverbs 4:23, it says, "more than all else, guard your heart, because from it are the bounds of your life." This is a very sobering thought: our thoughts (words) determine the bounds, or course, of our lives. Jesus spoke of "good and evil treasures of the heart" producing actions expressed in our words (Luke 6:45). The focus here is not so much on the externals (e.g., the use of foul language), but rather on the underlying condition of the human heart.

Finally, God is a God of language. His words are a living entity or being, which are His only begotten Son, the Christ. He speaks – the world is created, sustained or destroyed. Think of the power in this statement: God spoke everything into existence. There is no other religion or science with this belief and concept. God's breath, using His words, created life as we know it. Also, God's spoken word declares man's redemption through His Son, Jesus Christ.

Since the creation of mankind in the Garden of Eden, it's awesome to realize God created us to talk and walk with Him and to love like Him. It is amazing how humans alone are given the gift of language to talk to God and walk with him in full conversation while the rest of creation do not. What an awesome privilege we were given out of all creation to speak to God.

There are numerous Scriptures which expound on the power of words.

Proverbs 25:11 - 15:

"A word fitly spoken is like apples of gold in pictures of silver...By long forbearing is a prince persuaded, and a soft tongue breaketh the bone."

THIS LINE MUST BE REMOVED in PDF

Proverbs 18: 21:

"Death and life are in the power of the tongue: and they that love it shall eat the fruit thereof."

Proverbs 23:7:

"For as he thinketh in his heart, so is he: Eat and drink, saith he to thee; but his heart is not with thee."

Words are like a strong wind.

Job 8:2:

"How long wilt thou speak these things? and how long shall the words of thy mouth be like a strong wind?"

Words are deep waters.

Proverbs 18:4:

"The words of a man's mouth are as deep waters, and the wellspring of wisdom as a flowing brook."

The words of a tale bearer are as wounds.

Proverbs 18:8:

"The words of a talebearer are as wounds, and they go down into the innermost parts of the belly."

Since we know how utterly powerful words are, how are we to properly use them?

Seek to use words wisely. In Proverbs 15:2 it says, "The tongue of the wise useth knowledge aright: but the mouth of fools poureth out foolishness." We need to ask God for wisdom before we speak. He can teach us through His holy Word how to use words.

Have few words to say. "Be not rash with thy mouth, and let not thine heart be hasty to utter any thing before God: for God is in heaven, and thou upon earth: therefore let thy words be few" (Ecclesiastes 5:2). And again in Proverbs 10:19, "In the multitude of words there wanteth not sin: but he that refraineth his lips is wise."

Speak appropriately for the occasion. "A word fitly (speak appropriate for the occasion) spoken is like apples of gold in pictures of silver" (Proverbs 25:11).

Take heed to all words that are spoken. "Also take no heed unto all words that are spoken; lest thou hear thy servant curseth thee:" (Ecclesiastes 7: 20).

Some of the greatest words ever spoken were in Exodus 20:1-17 when God bade Moses to speak the Ten Commandments.

And God spake all these words, saying,

I am the Lord thy God, which have brought thee out of the land of Egypt, out of the house of bondage.

Thou shalt have no other gods before me.

Thou shalt not make unto thee any graven image, or any likeness of any thing that is in heaven above, or that is in the earth beneath, or that is in the water under the earth.

Thou shalt not bow down thyself to them, nor serve them: for I the Lord thy God am a jealous God, visiting the iniquity of the fathers upon the children unto the third and fourth generation of them that hate me;

And shewing mercy unto thousands of them that love me, and keep my commandments.

Thou shalt not take the name of the Lord thy God in vain; for the Lord will not hold him guiltless that taketh his name in vain.

Remember the sabbath day, to keep it holy.

Six days shalt thou labour, and do all thy work:

But the seventh day is the sabbath of the Lord thy God: in it thou shalt not do any work, thou, nor thy son, nor thy daughter, thy manservant, nor thy maidservant, nor thy cattle, nor thy stranger that is within thy gates:

For in six days the Lord made heaven and earth, the sea, and all that in them is, and rested the seventh day: wherefore the Lord blessed the sabbath day, and hallowed it.

Honour thy father and thy mother: that thy days may be long upon the land which the Lord thy God giveth thee.

Thou shalt not kill.

Thou shalt not commit adultery.

Thou shalt not steal.

Thou shalt not bear false witness against thy neighbour.

Thou shalt not covet thy neighbour's house, thou shalt not covet thy neighbour's wife, nor his manservant, nor his maidservant, nor his ox, nor his ass, nor any thing that is thy neighbour's.

The state of maturity for the Seed of Truth regarding the Power of Words is the realization words have the power to bring life or death, good or bad, and to always use words wisely and for the glory of God.

Chapter Eleven
_____

Beauty

We all have this in common: we love and admire beautiful people and things. And of old it has been said, "beauty is in the eye of the beholder." True, holy beauty (i.e., beauty of the heart) is a character trait which transcends all humanity, thoughts, and judgments. True beauty radiates like the sun and is visible for all to see and behold. True beauty penetrates the human conscience, creating intense awareness and attraction to itself. It is so alluring and magnetic, one can only help but notice and be engulfed and enthralled by it.

St. Thomas Aquinas (an Italian Dominican friar, Catholic priest, and a very influential philosopher and theologian) said, "Characteristics which define beauty are *wholeness, harmony, and radiance*. The being of all things is derived from divine beauty." This is beauty in a state of maturity.

The Hebrew root word for *beauty* is **yaphah**, which means to be bright; (by implication) be (make self) fair(-r); to deck. The Psalmist in Psalm 45: 11 said, "So shall the king greatly desire thy beauty: for he is thy Lord; and worship thou him."

As humans, we can only desire something visible. If our inward beauty is not visible to others and to God, it is not mature. Then we are in need of growth in this Truth.

Few can say their life is full of beauty. At its beginning (seed form), beauty is a faint flicker, a tiny ray of light. In its infancy, beauty is barely noticeable. However, even as a glimmer or sparkle, it is a sign of what is possible.

Who does not love or enjoy full, bright light? It warms the heart and encourages the soul, filling it with hope, love, and peace.

Growing into full maturity in the Truth regarding beauty is a process. It requires a high degree of consciousness, transparency, and unbridled Truth. Few are ready for the light to shine so bright to reveal all blemishes, faults, errors, sins, trespasses, transgressions, and iniquities. Even in the natural, too much light can be debilitating and harmful. And since beauty emanates from light, our character and personality must grow accustomed to more light to take on more beauty.

Beauty, in the state of immaturity, is like a faint flicker of a candle which only gives light in a small measure. Those walking in the path of dim light will struggle to see how to clearly walk in confidence, boldness, love, and assurance.

The state of maturity for the Seed of Beauty is our light becomes brighter so beauty can radiate through our countenance, personality, and deeds as a light to lead and encourage others in the way of Truth.

_____

Chapter Twelve

Love

Love is such a force of nature whether in seed form or maturity. Of all the characteristics of God, love is the greatest. For mankind, the full mature state of love is to love the Lord with all our heart, mind, and soul. Then love ourselves and our neighbor (i.e., other people in general).

The Bible says, "No greater love than this is a man who will lay down his life for a friend. Mature love is laying down yourself and lifting up another person. Mature love is loving a spouse like Christ loves the church. Mature love focuses on the good in self and others. Mature love forgives. Mature love avoids wronging others and always seeks to do the right thing in every circumstance or situation. Mature love overlooks faults so as not to judge another.

If the seed of love has taken root and grown, we do not allow hatred and scorn to rule in our lives. If love has not sufficiently grown in our heart, we struggle to put the will of God and the need of others above our own. But when love begins to grow in our heart, a world of possibility opens and as Paul wrote in 1 Corinthians 13:

> Though I speak with the tongues of men and of angels, and have not charity [i.e., love], I am become as sounding brass, or a tinkling cymbal.
>
> And though I have the gift of prophecy, and understand all mysteries, and all knowledge; and though I have all faith, so that I could remove mountains, and have not charity, I am nothing.
>
> And though I bestow all my goods to feed the poor, and though I give my body to be burned, and have not charity, profiteth me nothing.
>
> Charity suffereth long, and is kind; charity envieth not; charity vaunteth not itself, is not puffed up,
>
> Doth not behave itself unseemly, seeketh not her own, is not easily provoked, thinketh no evil;
>
> Rejoiceth not in iniquity, but rejoiceth in the truth;
>
> Beareth all things, believeth all things, hopeth all things, endureth all things.
>
> Charity never faileth: but whether there be prophecies, they shall fail; whether there be tongues, they shall cease; whether there be knowledge, it shall vanish away.
>
> For we know in part, and we prophesy in part.
>
> But when that which is perfect is come, then that which is in part shall be done away.

> When I was a child, I spake as a child, I understood as a child, I thought as a child: but when I became a man, I put away childish things.
>
> For now we see through a glass, darkly; but then face to face: now I know in part; but then shall I know even as also I am known.
>
> And now abideth faith, hope, charity, these three; but the greatest of these is charity.

If we are still like sounding brass or tinkling cymbal, have nothing of spiritual value to share with others, impatient, mean spirited, jealous, boasting, selfish, proud, eager to believe a lie then our love is not mature.

Finally, perfect love casts out all fear. Mature love no longer fears, because there is nothing to fear when you love with all your heart. Thomas a Kempis (a German-Dutch canon during the medieval period) said, "He who loves God with all his heart dreads neither death, torment, judgment, nor hell, for perfect love opens a sure passage to God."

The state of maturity for the Seed of Truth regarding Love is patience, faith, hope, endurance, strength, and no fear.

When love becomes our greatest motive for everything we do and say, we know we have reached maturity. Jan Van Ruysbroeck said, "our work is the [very] love of God."

Chapter Thirteen

Believing

For this seed of Truth, we will examine why believing is so fundamental to the Christian life. Believing is vastly more than mental assent to something or someone. Believing also involves a commitment of the will and an investment of one's heart, soul, and material substances.

Hebrews 11:6 (AMP) says,

But without faith it is impossible to please and be satisfactory to Him. For whoever would come near to God must (necessarily) believe that God exists and that He is the Rewarder of those who earnestly and diligently seek Him (out).

According to an ancient proverb, "For those who believe, no proof is necessary. For those who don't believe no proof is possible." (*The Encyclopedia of Christian Quotes*)

Why is it impossible to please God without believing? When you believe in God, then you trust, submit, confide, and respect Him. Without these things, a relationship cannot be established nor maintained. Without a relationship, there is no fellowship and no long-term interaction and exchange of ideas. And two lives cannot be united.

Quite simply, you have to believe in the character of a person to walk with them any distance. "Can two walk together, except they be agreed? (Amos 3:3 - KJV). To be agreed, there must be a common belief or a shared value system in things important between two people.

Ellen G. White, author of the *Desire of Ages*, opined faith is not in allegiance to presumption—they are not one and the same. "Only he who has true faith is secure against presumption. For presumption is Satan's counterfeit of faith. Faith claims God's promises, and brings forth fruit in obedience."

What does believing look like as a mature Christian? Let's look at several examples in the Bible. The Apostle Paul is such an example. He said, "Wherefore, sirs, be of good cheer: for I believe God, that it shall be even as it was told me." Like Paul, if you are mature in your belief, if God says it, there is absolutely no further need of encouragement or seeking affirmation to verify if it is so. However, an immature Christian will continue to doubt, second guess, and seek affirmation from God or others until they are satisfied God told them to do something whether big or small. Paul even said, you can be of good cheer when God tells you something. There is no reason to doubt, fear, or be sad.

There is much need of growth in this area for most Christians. The present, secular world has aggressively attacked Truth and viciously discredited Christ and God. This has caused Christians to be afraid to stand-up for and stand on God's Word and profess the Truth. But now is the time to believe more than ever. We must declare like the Apostle Paul "Wherefore . . . I believe even as it was told me."

Ignorance is the greatest hindrance to believing in God. Ignorance about His nature is the root of doubt and unbelief. When you know a person you trust like a spouse, friend, or relative, you no longer or seldom doubt their intentions or ability to do what they promise. So it is with God. We must begin to believe in His nature. And we do this by learning of Him through His Holy Word, the Bible.

Another example is Abraham "For what saith the scripture? Abraham believed God, and it was counted unto him for righteousness" (Romans 4:3). Righteousness is right thinking, feeling, and doing the right things pertaining to and related to God. So, when we believe that is the beginning of our being righteous.

And as we grow to maturity, our tree of belief is strong and mighty.

Psalm 1:1 – 3 confirms this:

Blessed is the man that walketh not in the counsel of the ungodly, nor standeth in the way of sinners, nor sitteth in the seat of the scornful.

But his delight is in the law of the Lord; and in his law doth he meditate day and night.

And he shall be like a tree planted by the rivers of water, that bringeth forth his fruit in his season; his leaf also shall not wither; and whatsoever he doeth shall prosper.

The state of maturity for the Seed of Believing is we become a tree planted by rivers of water in God's Word.

I encourage you to grow this seed of Truth to maturity and be like a strong tree planted by rivers of water by God's Word. And no wind or storm can uproot you in your love relationship with God.

Chapter Fourteen

Brokenness

Those of us who have experienced brokenness of any form knows it can be painful and debilitating. However, what we may not know or be fully aware is those who are broken are precious in the sight of the Lord Jesus Christ. When as immature Christians we don't realize this Truth, we despair of our brokenness and can live in depression and constant defeat. But we don't have to despair in our brokenness for God is near such suffering from a broken heart and contrite spirit. The remedy or cure for brokenness is the Lord Jesus Christ and being part of the Body of Christ, which is the church.

Oscar Wilde, humbled by this plight, aptly said, "How else but through a broken heart may Lord Christ enter in." (*The New Encyclopedia of Christian Quotations*)

Brokenness takes many forms, and we all have experienced it in our lives at one point or another.

Some experience emotional, sexual, social, relational, or financial brokenness.

I am convinced our brokenness is merely an invitation for healing from the Lord Jesus Christ and acceptance into the Body of Christ. We can trade our brokenness, or ashes so to speak, for Christ's beauty. In our state of immaturity when we don't know, believe, and act on this, we become discouraged. But God has provided healing for our brokenness through His Son and the Body of Christ.

There are plenty of scriptures to support this prin-ciple. First, in Psalm 34:18, it says, "The Lord is **nigh** unto them that are of a broken heart; and **saveth** such as be of a contrite spirit." And in Psalm 51:17, the passage says, "The sacrifices of God are a broken spirit: a broken and a contrite heart, O God, thou wilt not despise."

Moreover, Isaiah 57:15 says, "For thus saith the high and lofty One that inhabiteth eternity, whose name is Holy; I dwell in the high and holy place, with him also that is of a contrite and humble spirit**, to revive the spirit of the humble, and to revive the heart of the contrite ones**."

Finally, Isaiah 66: 2 opines, "For all those things hath mine hand made, and all those things have been, saith the Lord: **but to this man will I look,** even to him that is poor and of a contrite spirit, and trem-bleth at my word."

So, as scripture clearly shows, God not only saves the broken, but he dwells with them and looks after

them. Part of how He does this is through His Word
and the Body of Christ.

In 1 Corinthians 12:22 - 25:

Nay, much more those members of the body,
which seem to be more feeble, are necessary:

And those members of the body, which we
think to be less honourable, upon these we
bestow more abundant honour; and our uncomely
parts have more abundant comeliness.

For our comely parts have no need: but God
hath tempered the body together, having given
more abundant honour to that part which lacked:

That there should be no schism in the body;
but that the members should have the same care
one for another.

In the Body of Christ, those who are broken and
feeble are to be given **more abundant honor and
more abundant comeliness**. This is such a beautiful principle of Truth: in our need and lack, of
varying degrees, we get more abundant honor and
comeliness. It almost does not seem fair or hardly an
even trade to give the Lord our need and brokenness
in exchange for great abundance! But I can assure
you, this is the case. Our Heavenly Father is so loving
and caring, He provides for our every need.

Let's examine a little closer the meaning of *honor*
and *comeliness* and what we get in exchange for surren-
dering brokenness to the Lord. The word *honor* in
Hebrew has several meanings, but the word ***yaqar***

(pronounced yaw'kar), gives the best meaning and connotation in my opinion. **Yaqar** means to make rare; be (make) precious; be prized; withdraw [from brokenness]. And **yaqar** derives from the root word **yaqar (pronounced yaw'kawr)**, which means brightness, clear, costly, excellent, precious, reputation.

There are also several Greek words for *honorable*, but the one word which captures the essence of them all is **entimos (pronounced en'tee'mos)**, which means valued; dear; precious, in reputation.

We still have to define *comeliness*, which in the Hebrew is the word **hadar (pronounced haw'-dawr)** , which means magnificence, i.e. ornament or splendor; beauty; excellency; glorious; glory; goodly; honour; majesty. **Howd (pronounced hode)** is another Hebrew word for *comeliness*, and it means essentially the same as **hadar**, which expands the meaning to grandeur (i.e. an imposing form and appearance).

Comeliness in the Greek is the word **euschemon (pronounced yoo'skhay'mone)**, which means well-formed, i.e. (figuratively) decorous, noble (in rank); comely, honourable.

What a beautiful and glorious picture we get from these meanings of honorable and comeliness! No wonder one can doubt simply trading brokenness can yield such wonderful and marvelous things and station in life. But it is true, because God cannot lie--His Word is true. Therefore, to experience this great transformation (albeit progressive), we must recognize the Truth, believe it, and walk in it. And for most of us, this transformation will be a process. But as we mature, we will see a gradual change in our hearts and mind. The Truth will make (implying it is a process) us free from brokenness! Jesus proclaimed the transforming power of Truth in John 8:32, "And ye shall know the truth, and the truth shall make you free." To "make" something is a process, not a one-time event or experience. So, patience is needed, but the results are worth waiting for.

Because God is so loving and caring for the broken, the Apostle Paul was able to proclaim, "Not that I speak in respect of want: for I have learned, in whatsoever state I am, therewith to be content" (Philippians 4:11). He also was confident in that he also boasted, "And he said unto me, My grace is sufficient for thee: for my strength is made perfect in weakness. Most gladly therefore will I rather glory in my infirmities, that the power of Christ may rest upon me" (2 Corinthian 12:9).

If after reading God's holy Word and what it says about brokenness and we continue to doubt, it is a sure sign of immaturity and indicates the need for growth in this Truth. Maturity does not doubt God's Word. However, "Faith lives in a broken heart. True faith always grows in a heart humbled for sin, in a weeping eye and a tearful conscience" (Thomas Watson, *The New Encyclopedia of Christian Quotations*).

The state of maturity from brokenness is we no longer think weakness is weakness. But we realize and appreciate the fact God is our saving strength and will undoubtedly bestow beauty (honor and comeliness) for ashes as we surrender our brokenness to Him.

"God can do wonders with a broken heart: if we give him all the pieces." (Author unknown, *The New Encyclopedia of Christian Quotations)*

Concluding Thoughts

Unfortunately, the following poem is from an unknown author—he certainly deserves credit and public recognition for such revealing, inspiring thoughts on growth. It is a beautiful summation of my work.

Sometimes we must be hurt in order to grow,
We must fail in order to know,
We must lose in order to gain,
Some lessons are learned best
only through pain.
Sometimes our vision clears,
Only after our eyes are washed with tears.
Sometimes we have to be broken,
So we can be tender;
Sick, so we can rest and think better
On things more important than work or fun;
Trip near death,
so we can assess how we've run.

Sometimes we have to suffer lack,
So we can know God's provisions.
Feel another's pain,
So we can have a sense of mission.
So take heart, my friend,
If you don't understand today,
Instead of grumbling,
ask God what he means to say [in prayer].
In order to learn, you must endure
And learn to see the bigger picture.
In order to grow, you must stand
Look beyond the hurt, to God's loving hand
That takes what is good
And gives what is best
And on this blessed thought: rest.
As your anxious heart, with questions: wait.
God's hand only gives, what his loving
heart dictates.

I encourage—no, I insist—you get alone with God to meditate and reflect on Truths, which are central to the Christian life and watch the transformation in your faith and level of growth in every aspect of life.

Get a vision of each seed of Truth you want to plant and grow. Then believe and begin nurturing it until fruition. You will be amazed how quickly Truth grows in a fertile heart and mind.

God is no respecter of person, which means He is not partial or favors one person over another. As you commune with Him, He is faithful to reveal Himself and His Truth to you--personally. It is an awesome opportunity to get the revelation of the Word directly from God's Throne Room in Heaven. There is no substitute for a personal relationship with the Lord Jesus Christ and the Heavenly Father.

Finally, as the Apostle Peter admonished the church in his day: "But grow in grace [undeserved favor, spiritual strength] and recognition and knowledge and understanding of our Lord and Savior Jesus Christ, the Messiah. To Him [be] glory [honor, majesty and splendor] both now and to the day of eternity. Amen—so be it!" (2 Peter 3:18 AMP).

And as you begin your journey to grow, I pray the Hebrew Blessing upon you.

Numbers 6:24 - 26 (KJV):
    The Lord bless thee, and keep thee:
    The Lord make his face shine upon thee, and be gracious unto thee:
    The Lord lift up his countenance upon thee, and give thee peace.

About the Author

Donald Woods is a retired international trade Executive after 34 years and an author. He is an avid Bible student and lay minister at Christ Gospel Churches International. Donald served in the U.S. Air Force for 12 years. He is married (wife Mary) and has two beautiful daughters (Kyrah Marie and Nia Cheyenne) and lives in the Southern Indiana area. Donald has a Bachelor's and Master of Science degree in Business Administration and Management, respectively, from Indiana Wesleyan University.

You may contact him at donjwoods@icloud.com.

www.ingramcontent.com/pod-product-compliance
Lightning Source LLC
Chambersburg PA
CBHW031631040426
42452CB00007B/776